The Stone

That the

Builders
Rejected

The Lord told me that Psalm 23
is my blanket for protection during the day
and at night He tucks me in with it.

Pastor Alverna Brown Walker Graham

ISBN 979-8-88832-424-0 (paperback)
ISBN 979-8-88832-425-7 (digital)

Christian Faith Publishing
832 Park Avenue
Meadville, PA 16335
www.christianfaithpublishing.com

All scripture given is from the King James Version.

Printed in the United States of America

*Jesus said unto them, Did ye never read in the
scriptures, the stone that the builders rejected,
the same is become the head of the corner:
this is the Lord's doing, and it is marvelous in our eyes?*

—Matthew 21:42

CONTENTS

FOREWORD

I have been honored to have collaborated with Alverna on the story of her life.

We have been friends for over twenty-three years, and I have known her humanity, her heart, her humility, and her hopes.

I pray that her story will inspire and encourage the reader to surrender their life to God and see what He will do for them!

Linda S. Canaday

PREFACE

After the writing of my first book I realized that there had to be a sequel. While my first book was still at the publishers, I was writing the second by the guidance of the Holy Spirit.

One of my prayer partners said to me that there were "books" inside that first book after she had read it.

There were many others who said the same thing after they had also read it, which was also confirmed to me.

At the book signing of *Look What the Lord Has Done*, it was hard to describe the experience of the peace and the presence of the anointing there on my deck. It was more than a book signing; there was much ministry going forth that Saturday. The Lord had instructed me to hold that event at my home, and I did exactly as He said. It was to be a one to four o'clock drop-in, but most people just stayed the rest of the afternoon some even stayed until six o'clock.

Someone came and told me that I was an ambassador. I had previously been told that by another prophet. The weather was perfect! Leading up to the event, it had rained every day, so I asked the Lord not to let it rain that day. He said, *Have I ever let you down?* No, Lord, I replied. It rained hard in other places on the island that day, but not at my home.

Look what the Lord has done again!

It felt like we were having *real* church that day! God's peace hovered over that event!

I want to dedicate this work to the Holy Spirit, who is my faithful friend, guidance, counselor, advocate, and direction. He teaches me and helps me to walk in truth. He gives me blessings and gifts of the Holy Spirit.

I want to leave a legacy to my children, grandchildren, and great-grandchild.

Children

Annette
Bridget
Katina
Terry
Damon
Rollins

Grandchildren

Lauren
London
Karrington
Brooke
Larsyn

Great-Grandchild

Nile

In the writing of this second book, I have had to look back over all that I have lived through even as a little child—the good, the bad, and the ugly. Through all the times and all the trials, I can see how God's hand was on me from the beginning, for a time and a purpose that hasn't been completed yet.

ACKNOWLEDGMENTS

The Brown Family
The Rose Family
The Nelson Family
Patricia J. Poole Porcher
Olivia Richardson and Family
Doris Johnson Ministry
Linda S. Canaday
Sea Island Habitat for Humanity
John's Island (South Carolina, 29455)

CHAPTER 1

The Separation of My Siblings

The enemy was working overtime in my family. A lot of heartache, disappointment, and rejection. The enemy used my siblings against me in many ways, but I knew that God was still with us. Even though I took care of my siblings at an early age, I counted them as my own children instead of siblings during that time because I was the oldest in the home. The enemy always attacks the weaker vessel and plays on their mind.

God reminded me, "Dearly beloved avenge not your selves, but rather give place unto wrath: for it is written, vengeance is mine; I will repay, saith the Lord" (Romans 12:19).

He told me to keep on trusting Him with my life, and He will work it out.

> Trust in the Lord with all thine heart;
> and lean not unto thine own understanding.
> (Proverbs 3:5)

> Trust in the Lord and do good. (Psalm 37:3)

> Commit thy way unto the Lord; trust also
> in Him; and He will bring it to pass. (Psalm 37:5)

He said it in Matthew 5:44: "But I say unto you, love your enemies, bless them that curse you, and pray for them who despitefully use you and persecute you."

I will always be there for my siblings when they need me, and the enemy cannot turn me away from them because God put families together to build one another up and not to tear one another down.

The enemy works overtime to tear it apart. He attacks me on every hand, but I say to those, "I am doing a great work so that I cannot come down" (Nehemiah 6:3).

For unto whomsoever much is given, of
him shall much be required. (Luke 12:48)

I have to forgive everyone who is involved because I know that is of God. "For if ye forgive men their trespasses, your heavenly Father will also forgive you" (Matthew 6:14). The old cliché says that sticks and stones will break your bones, but words will never hurt you. But words do hurt you.

I don't look like what I have been through.

I am not defined by what has been *done to me*, but I am defined by what has been *done for me* at the cross.

Some of my siblings try to turn my children against one another; that spirit was spilling over into my children's lives; but I cursed it from the root, and that was where it stopped!

Now God has moved in our lives, and we have a better relationship with one another. They call me for prayer and counseling when they need it.

A woman of God visited me one day and reminded me of my first set of children, who were my siblings. I had never seen it that way before; I only saw hardship. I cried after she left because of what I was going through at that time when caring for my siblings. I was my siblings' caregiver at the early age of seven. My youngest sister didn't even know our mother as she was only six months old when Mother passed. She called me *mama* when she started talking. My youngest brother was four, and my other sister was five years old.

I raised my mother's children, and when I finished, God finished raising me.

> And we know that all things work together
> for good to them that love God, to them who are
> called according to His purpose. (Romans 8:28)

God never throws anything away—the hurts, the tears, the hard times, the long and dry times, sickness, pain, lack. God uses all these things to grow us, strengthen us, temper us, refine us, define us, and fine-tune us.

> The stone that the builders rejected, the
> same is become the head of the corner: this is
> the Lord's doing, and it is marvelous in our eyes.
> (Matthew 21:42)

God spoke to me years ago that I would go to the nations. Thus far, I have visited Ghana, Africa; Lima, Peru; and Tokyo, Japan. Now He is sending me different nationalities to be ministered to.

He has opened doors for me to go into different areas such as Seabrook Island, Kiawah Island, and the Charleston area. In this journey, I never thought I would be so accepted in so many people's lives. I've been rejected for so long that the acceptance of so many different types of people have been overwhelming at times, from the haters to the people who really love and care for you. At the same time, I want to thank my haters because they helped usher me into the destiny where God is taking me.

When I became an adult and surrendered my life to Jesus Christ, He told me that He had made a promise to my mother that He would take care of us through the hard times and the good times. He never failed us. He was always with us up to this time, and He is still with us. God's anointing is heavy upon us. Every time I think of my father and mother, God allows me to feel His presence upon me.

> In thy presence is fullness of joy, at thy right hand there are pleasures for ever more. (Psalm 16:11)

God also reminded me of these scriptures:

> My latter days will be greater than my beginning. (Job 8:7)

> For I know the thoughts I think towards you, said the Lord, thoughts of peace and not of evil, to give you an expected end. (Jeremiah 29:11)

I have a good relationship with all of my nieces and nephews. They respect me to the highest, and when some of them come into town, they come by to see me. That is a blessing from God. Because you will reap what you sow. "Be not deceived; God is not mocked; for whatsoever a man soweth, that shall he also reap" (Galatians 6:7). I will always stand in the gap and pray for the salvation of my family because I have a charge to keep and a God to glorify. Family is very important to God.

> No weapon that is formed against thee shall prosper: and every tongue that shall rise against thee in judgement thou shalt condemn. This is the heritage of the servants of the Lord, and their righteousness is of Me, saith the Lord. (Isaiah 54:17)

> What shall we say to these things? If God be for us, who can be against us? (Romans 8:31)

> They that sow in tears shall reap in joy. He
> that goeth forth weepeth, bearing precious seed,
> shall doubtless come again with rejoicing, bring-
> ing his sheaves with him. (Psalm 126:5–6).

Psalm 56 says that God put David's tears in his bottle; God does the same for us.

The devil whispered in my ear, "You're not strong enough to withstand the storm." I whispered in the devil's ear, "I AM THE STORM." When you bring my past up, you have to go to hell to get it.

> I can do all things through Christ which
> strengtheneth me. (Philippians 4:13)

My journey of the past gives me hope for the future. There is purpose in the pain. Setbacks in life can be used by God as a setup for blessing. I focus on His presence in my life and not the pain I suffered. God will not remove the pain to bless you and me. Call Him up; His phone number is Jeremiah 33:3:

> There were people that had a bad influence
> on my siblings; God said that they would pay.
> Vengeance is mine, saith the Lord.

My siblings and I remind me of the story of Joseph and his brothers. "But as for you, ye thought evil against me, but God meant it unto good, to bring to pass, as it is this day, to save much people alive" (Genesis 50:20). I understood better what I was going through. It was a very bad experience for me—the jealousy, the lies, and the plotting that other people were telling my siblings about me that separated us from one another. They threw the bricks and hid their hands. They came after me through my siblings, but I will always stand up to my enemies in a godly way.

Each family is blessed to have one another, to build one another up and not tear them down. God said that He will let me see the wrath on my enemies who have tried to destroy me. And I am seeing some of that now.

> Who shall lay anything to the charge of GOD's elect? It is GOD that justified. (Romans 8:33)

> Thy word is a lamp unto my feet, and a light unto my path. (Psalm 119:105)

> It is good for me that I have been afflicted that I might learn Thy statutes. (Psalm 119:71)

I didn't realize how broken I was until I started writing these books and God showed me different things that hurt me in my life that were still there. There are some things I didn't want to address, but I had to get naked before God and let Him know how I was hurting. Of course, God already knew that, but He wanted me to admit and verbalize it to Him.

> In Thy presence is fulness of joy: at Thy right hand there are pleasures for evermore. (Psalm 16:11b)

> God also reminded me that my latter days would be greater than my beginning. (Job 8:7)

> For I know the thoughts that I think toward you, saith the Lord, thoughts of peace and not of evil, to give you an expected end. (Jeremiah 29:11)

> I know both how to be abased, and I know how to abound: every where and in all things I am instructed both to be full and be hungry, both to abound and to suffer need. I can do all things through Christ which strengtheneth me. (Philippians 4:12–13)

CHAPTER 2

The Separation from My Husband

When my husband and I first got married, we had a good relationship with each other until he allowed the enemy of alcohol to overtake him in our relationship. Things started going downhill from that time until we separated. He was my assignment, but I didn't know it at the time; I realized that later in the marriage when I received a phone call from one of my prayer partners, letting me know that the marriage was more for my husband than me. God wanted to prepare my husband to become a great man of God, but the alcohol kept him from surrendering all to the Lord Jesus Christ. The enemy was working through my husband to sabotage the ministry that God had given me. "Because greater is He that is in you, than he that is in the world" (1 John 4:4b).

God would allow him and me to take communion daily; that instruction was for me to do that until God told me to stop, and that led up to the separation and to stop praying for him. God told Jeremiah three times to stop praying for His people in chapters 7, 11, and 14 in the book of Jeremiah. Shortly after that, God told me to have him leave the home.

One night when I was in prayer, I heard the voice of the Lord saying that it was time for him to leave. I told him the next morning when he came home from work, because he worked at night. God gave me such a peace about that decision. He gave me the assurance that He would take care of me in every situation. I felt such a peace in my soul that my body felt numb—no anxiety, no fear, such a peace that it is hard to put into words. Jesus said it best in John 14:7: "Peace I leave with you, My peace I give unto you; not as the world giveth give I unto you. Let not your heart be troubled, neither let it be afraid."

My husband didn't move immediately, but then decided to get up and leave the house. A couple of hours later, he returned and started packing his belongings. There was no conversation between us as he was gathering his stuff, except that while he was gone those couple of hours, I washed all his dirty clothes, had them folded and put aside for him until he returned. He thanked me for doing that.

> The peace of God which passeth all under-
> standing shall keep your hearts and minds
> through Christ Jesus. (Philippians 4:7)

He left on February 28, 2020, and I was scheduled for surgery three days later on March 3, 2020. God was still watching over me. After the surgery, He protected me during the time of my healing process with peace in my heart and my home. My healing was fast and complete. "The blessing of the Lord, it maketh rich, and He addeth no sorrow with it" (Proverbs 10:22). I am reminded of the song "There is a balm in Gilead" (a balm is a spiritual medicine).

The ladies from the Bible study group that I had been attending brought me a hot home-cooked meal every day for two weeks. It makes me cry just thinking about that. The favor of God is still on me. His promises are *yea* and *amen*.

My husband's sisters also offered to help after my surgery. They always felt more like sisters than sisters-in-law. The whole family treated me like family.

After a year of separation and no communication between me and my husband, I called his sister to tell her of some important mail that had come to the house for him that needed attention right away. He did come by to pick it up, and there was pleasant conversation between the two of us. God promised me that He was going to take care of him and that he was in God's hands. I saw the result of God's promise.

> God is not a man that He should lie. (Numbers 23:19)

Words Spoken to Me Directly by the Holy Spirit

After the separation, God told me that my haters are watching me and how I will handle this: "I am going to cover you with more anointing, more power, and more tenacity for ministry. I allowed you to go through this because I knew that you wouldn't quit or walk away from Me, and I can trust you," said the Lord. "I am pleased with you and your determination to stand."

> Howbeit when the Spirit of truth is come, He will guide you into all truth: for He shall not speak of Himself; but whatsoever He shall hear, that shall He speak: and He will show you things to come. (John 16:13)

CHAPTER 3

My Biological Parents

My dad, David Brown Jr., was named after David in the Bible, who was a man after God's own heart. "The Lord hath sought Him a man after His own heart" (1 Samuel 13:14). My dad only had a sixth-grade education but functioned as though he had a college degree. He was an architect, a brick mason, a commercial shrimper, a gardener, and a professional cook. He even built the house we lived in—a very gifted man! He was a sharp dresser also. I remember seeing him always shining his shoes. He always kept a sharp crease in his khaki pants, whether he was at home or going out. He didn't iron the crease in his pants; he folded them and put them under the mattress where we slept.

He was always devoted to his children. It was hard for him to work full-time, leaving his little children in the care of the oldest child, who was only seven years old. He was trying to be father and mother at the same time in caring for us after our mother died. It was so overwhelming for him that it escalated his drinking. When I look back over his accomplishments and how he did things, I consider him a very smart man.

One of the interesting things about my father was the generational birthmark of blessing that he carried. This mark was passed down from generation to generation. It was a patch of gray hair somewhere on the body. I can go back as far as five generations to my knowledge that had this mark. It skipped my children and showed up on my grandchildren.

During the time that I worked for the Department of Social Services, my supervisor, Ms. Gathers, called me into her office one day and asked me some questions about me and my family. She wanted to know who my family was because her maiden name was Brown also. I told her that my mother was deceased and that I was the oldest child in the home.

She asked me some questions about my father. That was hard to talk about, but I was led by the Holy Spirit to let her know that my father was sick with alcohol addiction. That's when she asked if I had any life insurance on him because he lived a careless life. I told her no, so she said that I needed to take some life insurance out on him. She called an insurance company from Columbia and set up an appointment with an agent to discuss putting life insurance on him, where it would be deducted out of my paycheck every two weeks. It was hard on me, but God supplied my needs!

About five years later, he passed away, and I was able to give him a good homegoing service with God's help. There was enough money left over to dress Jeanette, David, Emily, my children, and myself.

I found out while making the funeral arrangements for the burial of my father that two aunts had also put life insurance on him. One of the aunts told me while we were there at the funeral home that she was not going to contribute to the expenses. The second aunt didn't offer anything either. But God…

My girlfriend Olivia witnessed the arrangements and the conversation of my aunt. She has used this as a testimony and still talks about it to this day.

But God was still with us because He was our provider, and a large sum of money was left over after the burial, and all the expenses were paid in full. Look what the Lord has done again!

My supervisor, Ms. Gathers, imparted much wisdom to me about the burial of my father and how to get a Pell Grant for my children's college. She was a great teacher and mentor to me. At her homegoing service, I was asked to speak words of encouragement to her children, grandchildren, and family.

> Now unto Him that is able to do exceeding abundantly above all that we ask or think according to the power that worketh in us. (Ephesians 3:20)

I can remember some of the things that my father taught us as we were growing up. The most important thing that he taught us was the Lord's Prayer. He was building a foundation that would last us for the rest of our lives.

> Our Father which art in heaven
> Hallowed be THY Name
> THY kingdom come
> THY will be done
> On earth as it is in heaven
> Give us this day our daily bread
> And forgive us our debts
> As we forgive our debtors
> And lead us not into temptation
> But deliver us from evil
> For Thine is the kingdom
> and the power
> And the glory forever,
> Amen.
> (Matthew 6:9–11)

My mother, Althia Rose Brown, was a very attractive lady. I was told that she was mixed Cherokee Indian on her mother's side of the family. She had long jet-black hair. I have a mixture of looks. Some say that I look like my mother, and some say I look like my father. I can remember my great-grandmother Alvira had long hair and wore it in a braid that went all the way down her back. I remember that as if it was yesterday. One thing that I hated was getting my hair combed because it was thick and kinky, and it hurt so much that it made me cry.

My mother was a pleasant person. She had a sweet spirit in her. She was always hugging and kissing us. She loved her children very much.

One of our activities was picking up pecans together in my grandmother Agnes's yard on Wadmalaw Island.

I considered my mother as a Proverbs 31 woman:

> Who can find a virtuous woman? For her price is far above rubies. She will do him [her husband] good and not evil all the days of her life. She openeth her mouth with wisdom, and in her tongue is the law of kindness. Her children rise up and call her blessed; her husband also, and he praiseth her. Give her the fruit of her hands; and let her own works praise her in the gates. (Proverbs 31:12, 26, 28, 31)

She worked as a tomato checker at the local farms as much as she could because she had young children at home to care for while my dad was shrimping in Key West, Florida.

The day my mother passed was a Monday. I remember that because she kept me out of school that day so I could watch the baby while she went to John's Island. I remember what she wore that day: black pants and a white top.

She never made the trip that day because she passed with a massive heart attack at my cousin's house on Wadmalaw Island. She died December 9, and I believe it was 1957 (as best that I can remember). One of my cousins, Mr. Brown, came to my grandmother Agnes's house and gave her the news. I was right there when he told her that my mother had died. The feeling I had was unexplainable. I cried along with my grandmother.

My siblings were too young to comprehend what was going on. My mother was only twenty-five years old when she passed. On the day of the funeral, as we rode from downtown to the family church on John's Island, my grandmother held me in her arms, crying all the way to the church.

I even remember exactly what I wore that day: a gray-and-white outfit, gray dress with straps and a ruffled white blouse and black patent leather shoes.

After the service of my mother, as I was headed to the car to go back home to Wadmalaw Island, my oldest brother, Robert, ran toward me. He put his hand in his pocket and pulled out a handful of coins and gave them to me and gave me a big hug.

I give God all the glory and praise that we all have lived past that age. We are now in our sixties and seventies, except my oldest brother, who was in his fifties when he passed.

CHAPTER 4

The Eagle

The Lord told me that I am like an eagle: I fly high, and I don't eat any and everything. I pick and choose what to eat and what not to eat, naturally and spiritually.

The characteristics of an eagle are having keen eyes, being courageous, being strong willed, having great strength, being independent, being vocal, being competitive, and being shrewd. He is also known as the king of the skies, and that is the most specific place to be in for effective spiritual warfare—in high places in God.

An eagle is a very peculiar bird, and God calls us a peculiar people. "But ye are a chosen generation, a royal priesthood, an holy nation, a peculiar people; that that ye should show forth the praise of Him who hath called you out of darkness into His marvellous light" (1 Peter 2:9).

Eagles don't run from a storm in life; they run to it. As a storm approaches, they use the up drafts to take them above the storm. Eagles know how to ride the winds of God. In human life, these characteristics also make a good spouse and good parents. Christians and eagles have some of the same distinctive traits.

> But they that wait upon the Lord shall
> renew their strength, they shall mount up with
> wings as eagles, they shall run and not be weary,
> they shall walk and not faint. (Isaiah 40:31)

I have to stay focused and stay the course—without hinderance from anyone or anything. Nehemiah 6:3 says I am doing a great work, and I cannot come down. God said that if He be lifted up, He would draw all men unto Him. He said that in my prayer time: just lift Him up, and He would do the drawing.

God said that He is sending me to "deep fishing." Luke 5:4 reads, "Launch out into the deep, and let down your nets for a draught [a full catch]." My father was a deep-sea fisherman, and God is doing the same for me: sending me to dignitaries, millionaires, lawyers, doctors, nurses, rich and poor.

"To every thing there is a season, and a time to every purpose under the heaven" (Ecclesiastes 3:1). This is my season to go forth in the things of God and to pay close attention to the instruction He has given me. God thanked me for honoring Him through the story of my life. My real breakthrough came when I was not in churches but outside of the "church," in the privacy of my own home, which is a sanctuary that I dedicated to the Lord many years ago.

CHAPTER 5

Some Prophecies That Were Spoken Over My Life

Words Spoken to Me Directly by the Holy Spirit

Brethren, I count not myself to have apprehended: but this one thing I do, forgetting those things which are behind, and reaching forth unto those things which are before, I press toward the mark for the prize of
the high calling of God in Christ Jesus. (Philippians 3:13–14)

Let thine eyes look right on, let thine eyelids look straight before thee. Ponder the path of thy feet and let all thy ways be established. Turn not to the right hand nor to the left. (Proverbs 4:25–27)

God shall wipe away all tears from their eyes and there shall be no more death, neither sorrow, nor crying, neither shall there be any more pain: for the former things are passed away. (Revelation 21:4)

God said that I am the neck in the position to turn the heads of the leaders on John's Island area and throughout the nation.

> I am crucified with Christ; nevertheless I live; yet not I, but Christ liveth in me; and the life which I now live in the flesh, I live by the faith of the Son of God who loved me and gave Himself for me. (Galatians 2:20)

> The Spirit itself beareth witness with our spirit that we are the children of God. (Romans 8:16)

> And He said unto me, My Grace is sufficient for thee; for My strength is made perfect in weakness. (2 Corinthians 12:9)

> I can do all things through Christ which strengtheneth me. (Philippians 4:13)

> Therefore if any man be in Christ, he is a new creature; old things are passed away, all things are become new. (2 Corinthians 5:17)

The LORD will withhold no good thing for those who walk up rightly. Run the race that is set before us. I am doing more in the spiritual realm than can be seen in the natural. Every desire in one's heart is done. Believe it, and it will manifest in the natural. My word will not return to me void but will accomplish that to which I sent it.

Don't look to the left or to the right. Keep your eyes focused on Me. My thoughts are not your thoughts. After the storm comes promotion.

I AM THAT I AM. I am opening doors no man can shut. I am shutting doors no man can open. Believe the prophets, and you will prosper a great move in me, says the LORD.

Step out into the deep, cast your net out into the deep. Every prophetic word that was spoken over your life will come to pass over ministry. Yes, there is a shifting taking place, and I am in the midst of it. I am taking down some for this hour and raising some up, says the Lord.

The Lord told me many years ago, "I am going to make an example out of you," and that no person would get the glory out of my life, only God. He is my teacher. God told me not to be afraid of their faces, just speak His Word. He is taking me higher in His anointing. More is with me than against me. God said that He will contend with those who contend with me. I will operate in miracles, signs, and wonders under the anointing that He has placed on my life. God said that I have given myself to Him, and He has made me the head and not the tail, above and not beneath. He has given me more knowledge of His Word, more insight, and more influence on people. They have traveled miles and miles to connect with me or meet with me.

> Men shall call you ministers of our God. For your shame ye shall have double. And their seed shall be known among the Gentiles, and their offspring among the people; all that see them shall acknowledge them that they are the seed which the Lord has blessed. (Isaiah 61:6–7, 9)

He has given me grace to walk through this journey. A trip is short, but a journey is long! When the Lord told me that He was going to make an example out of me, you might think that, that sounded wonderful, but along with that came the pushing, pulling, pressure, and persecution.

More Words from Prophets

I am the one that opened the way through the waters, making a dry path through the sea. I call forth the mighty army of Pharaoh and drowned them in the water, but it is nothing compared to what

I am about to do; for I am doing a brand-new thing. This brand-new thing God is about to do is not going to be anything you have seen in the past.

We can all look back and see where God parted the Red Sea in our lives—where He opened up a door that shouldn't have opened and had us at the right place at the right time.

Get ready for something awesome that you haven't seen, something that propels you to a new level. When you see this new thing, you are going to stand in amazement and say, "Wow, look what the Lord has done!"

What seems impossible, He can make possible!

You're a queen; you're anointed! Nothing will happen to you because He has you covered. You don't have to worry about anything. (I had gone to my doctor's on the wrong day, but God had a nurse to give me a word while I was making a new appointment. She got up from her desk and came over to me to give me this word.)

Many Words Given to Me Over the Years by Prophets

God is sending angels to war on my behalf, and this is final. He is commanding favor on my life through the good times and the bad times. He constantly speaks peace in my life. He is sending good people to help me with ministry. I am the apple of His eye. God said that I am rock solid and unmovable. God can trust me with everything. He has increased my discernment in the spirit. He has loosed the ability to love the past, the present, and future.

God said that He is sending me to catch the hardest thing in the sea—that is, crabs. God is after *souls*! Fishers of men. God has already gathered the fish; just go get them. God requires me to jump, but He has me covered to jump into hard places and deep places where most people are afraid to go. He still has me covered with His anointing.

He that receiveth a prophet in the name
of a prophet shall receive a prophet's reward.
(Matthew 10:41)

> Believe in the Lord your God, so shall ye
> be established; believe His prophets, so shall ye
> prosper. (2 Chronicles 20:20)

Words from Prophets

The angel of the Lord said, "Tell my servant Alverna there is a mandate on her life to call in things. The Lord is calling you forth for intense and constant believing prayer from your heart, with some fasting that will cause the supernatural power of God to bring miraculous breakthrough in a given situation when you call a solemn assembly. He shall do it."

> But prayer was made without ceasing of the
> church unto God. (Acts 12:5)

God has sent four angels with gifts for each of us. (There were four people present at the chapel when this word was given.)

The walls are coming down!

In less than two weeks after the Lord said that my sister's house was going to be completely furnished by the Lord, a woman called her and told her that she was going to completely refurnish her home, down to the stove.

Each one of us has an assignment. Each born-again believer has been given an assignment, and it's what we do with that assignment that God has given to us. For example, when God told Noah to build an ark and how to do it when there was no rain in sight, Noah stayed focused when his critics tried to discourage him. When the flood came, all the critics were swept away.

When God gives you an assignment, it's very important that you follow through.

I will continue to work on my assignment that God has given to me. My assignment is to win souls for the kingdom of God.

To whom much has been given, much is required. He requires much of me because He has given me much!

I am crucified with Christ: nevertheless I live; yet not I, but Christ liveth in me: and the life which I now live in the flesh, I live by the faith of the Son of God, who loved me, and gave Himself for me. (Galatians 2:20)

That if thou shalt confess with thy mouth the Lord Jesus, and shalt believe in thine heart that God hath raised Him from the dead, thou shalt be saved. For with the heart man believeth unto righteousness, and with the mouth confession is made unto salvation. (Romans 10:9–10)

As you read these books that God has
downloaded in my spirit,
I hope that you
will make the same decision
that I made
to surrender my life to the
LORD JESUS CHRIST,
who is my personal Savior!

Before I formed thee in the belly I knew thee; and before thou camest forth out of the womb I sanctified thee and ordained thee a prophet unto the nations. (Jeremiah 1:5)

Ye have not chosen ME, but I have chosen you, and ordained you, that you should go and bring forth fruit, and that your fruit should remain: that whatsoever ye shall ask of the Father in my name, HE may give it you. (John 15:16)

ABOUT THE AUTHOR

Pastor Alverna Brown Walker Graham

After I gave my life to the LORD on February 23, 1991, GOD spoke to me audibly and said, "I am going to make an example out of you."

I had no idea what that meant! It has been an ongoing process in my life to this very day.

When persecution comes for His name sake, blessings always follow.

I have been ordained as a pastor, ministering in homeless shelters, prison, hospitals, speaking engagements, performing wedding ceremonies, funerals, and also helping others with their house churchs.

I am also on various bible study conference calls. I am ministering 24/7.

Recently God has been laying out books before me to write about what He has done and still yet doing in my life.

You are now reading the sequel to the first book.

"Look what the Lord has done"

And the best is still yet to come!